Mathematics
Level 1

Cherry Franklin, Chris Kitching,
Jamie McCulloch and Nicola Phair

Rising Stars UK Ltd.
22 Grafton Street, London W1S 4EX

www.risingstars-uk.com

Every effort has been made to trace copyright holders and obtain their permission for the use of copyright materials. The authors and publisher will gladly receive information enabling them to rectify any error or omission in subsequent editions.

All facts are correct at time of going to press.

Published 2009

Text, design and layout © 2009 Rising Stars UK Ltd.

The right of Cherry Franklin, Chris Kitching, Jamie McCulloch and Nicola Phair to be identified as the authors of this work has been asserted by them in accordance with the Copyright, Design and Patents Act 1998.

Authors: Cherry Franklin, Chris Kitching, Jamie McCulloch, Nicola Phair, Hazel Grove High School, Stockport
Consultant Maths Publisher: Jean Carnall
Text design and typesetting: Words & Pictures Ltd, London
Illustrator: Words & Pictures Ltd, London
Cover design: Burville-Riley Partnership

Photo acknowledgements
p.6 *luggage* iStockphoto; **p.7** *beach* Alexandr Ozerov/iStockphoto; **p.14** *smoothie* Julien Bastide/iStockphoto; **p.15** *window frame* iStockphoto, *smoothie* Olga Lyubkina/iStockphoto; **p.16** *strawberries* Stephen Rees/iStockphoto, *raspberries* Ken Pilon/iStockphoto; **p.17** *blackberries* Andrew Cribb/iStockphoto; **p.18** *scales* iStockphoto, *bananas* iStockphoto; **p.22** *grass* Aleksey Khromov/iStockphoto; **p.25** *blackboard* Olivier Blondeau/iStockphoto; **p.28** *newspaper cutting* Amanda Rohde/iStockphoto; **p.35** *hamburger* hywit dimyadi/iStockphoto, *lasagne* Barbro Bergfeldt/iStockphoto, *pizza* Vasko Miokovic/iStockphoto; **p.37** *corporate building* Ian Jeffery/iStockphoto; **p.44** *room* de santis paolo/iStockphoto

All rights reserved. No part of this publication may be reproduced, stored in a retrieval system, or transmitted, in any form by any means, electronic, mechanical, photocopying, recording or otherwise, without the prior permission of Rising Stars.

British Library Cataloguing in Publication Data.
A CIP record for this book is available from the British Library.

ISBN: 978-1-84680-629-2

Printed by Craft Print International Limited, Singapore

Contents

| **How to use** | 4 |

Unit 1 – Holidaying in Florida
A Planning a package	6
B Orlando weather	8
C Changing currency	10
D Scream Towers	12

Unit 2 – Smashing smoothies
A Re-writing recipes	14
B The price is right	16
C Units and measuring	18
D Which smoothie is best?	20

Unit 3 – At the match
A Groundsman	22
B The fan	24
C Kiosk manager	26
D Team manager	28

Unit 4 – Catering
A Market research	30
B The company premises	32
C Food and nutrition	34
D Public image of the company	36

Unit 5 – Bedroom makeover
A Choosing furniture	38
B Fitting in furniture	40
C Painting and decorating	42
D Designing pictures	44

Review exercises
Number and algebra	46
Shapes, space and measures	47
Handling data	48

How to use
About this book

Functional Skills is the name given to the areas of Mathematics (and English and ICT) that are needed when tackling real problems that you may come across in life and work. To help prepare for this, GCSE examinations and Diploma courses are changing to include more questions that focus on these types of problems. Functional Skills tests have also been introduced so that students can prove that they can solve longer, more realistic problems like those we face in real life.

This book will help you develop confidence and demonstrate Functional Skills at level 1.

The book is divided into five units, each of which has a central theme running through the questions. The units are further broken down into four parts. Each part is self contained so that you can work through the whole unit at one time or look at each part separately.

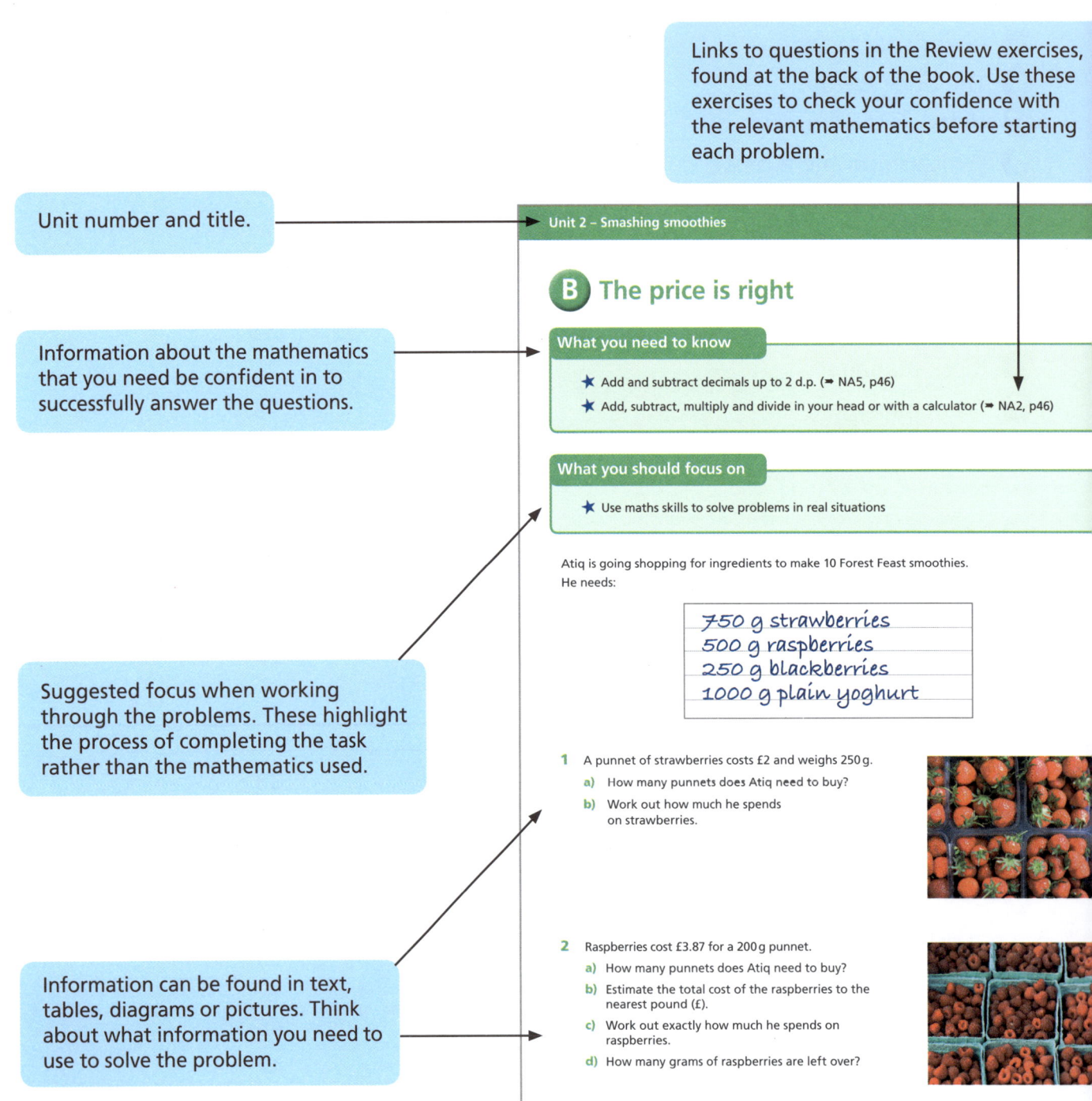

Links to questions in the Review exercises, found at the back of the book. Use these exercises to check your confidence with the relevant mathematics before starting each problem.

Unit number and title.

Information about the mathematics that you need be confident in to successfully answer the questions.

Suggested focus when working through the problems. These highlight the process of completing the task rather than the mathematics used.

Information can be found in text, tables, diagrams or pictures. Think about what information you need to use to solve the problem.

4

When tackling the problems you should:

★ Read the whole problem carefully, including all the questions and information. Get a feel for how the questions develop and what the overall problem is about.

★ Identify important information from the text, charts and diagrams.

★ Write down any decisions or assumptions you have made.

★ Plan how to answer the problem – some problems are structured to help you do this. Write down the stages you will work through to solve the problem.

★ Work through the stages you have planned, checking that your answers make sense as you go along.

★ Write down any calculations you have done.

★ Remember to write in any units that are needed. You can work out what these are from the problem. You won't be told to do this but you do need to include them so that your answer makes sense.

★ Write out your final answer in a sentence, explaining how you know it is correct.

★ When you've answered the problem, read the question again to check you've actually answered it.

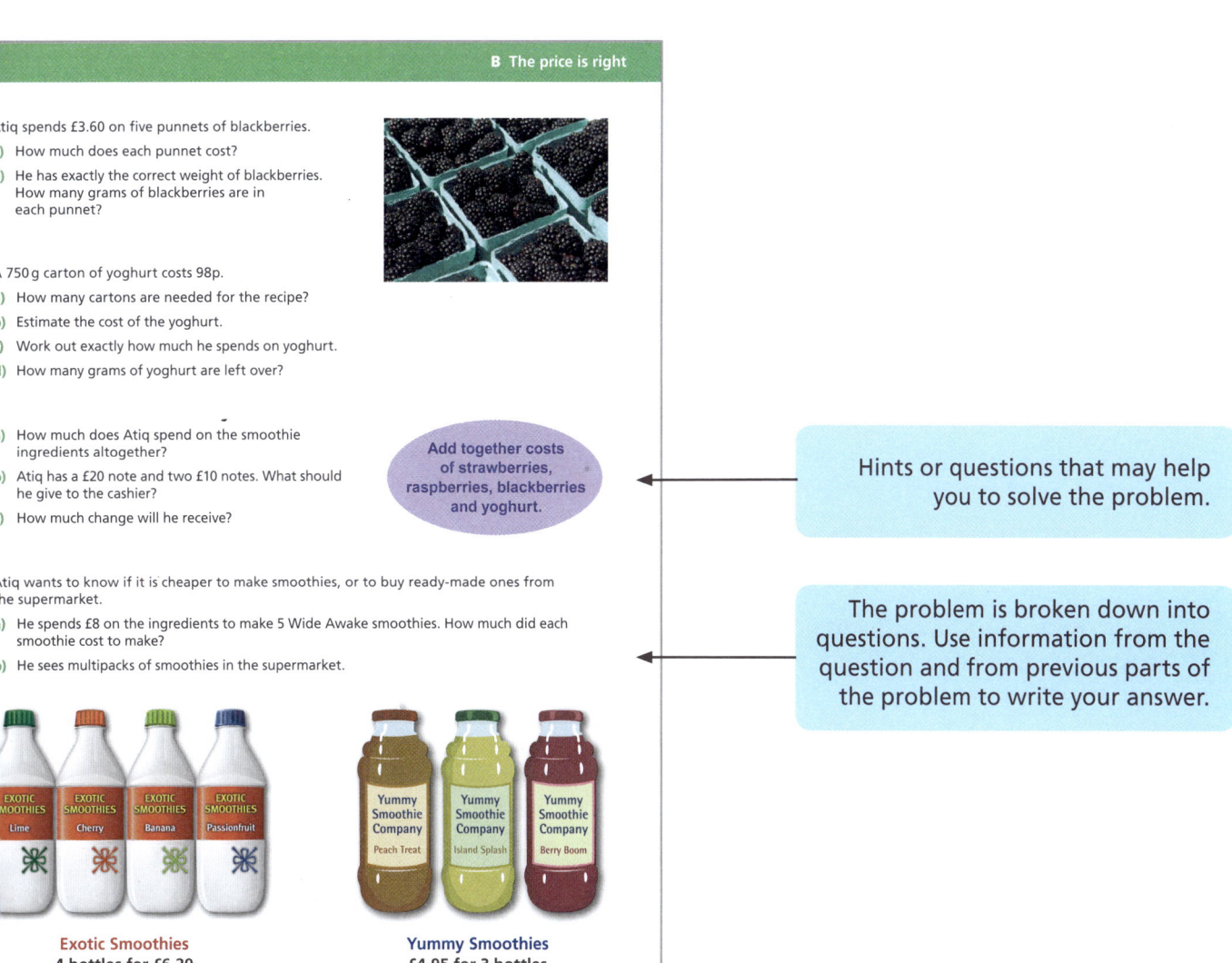

Unit 1 – Holidaying in Florida

 **A Planning a package**

What you need to know

★ Add, subtract, multiply and divide without a calculator (➡ NA2, p46)

★ Understand what different types of charts and graphs are showing you (➡ HD2, p48)

What you should focus on

★ Use maths skills to solve problems in real situations

1. Sarah is researching a family summer holiday to Florida for her mum, dad, brother and herself. She is considering the first two weeks of June. She first looks at return flights to Florida.

   a) How much does it cost for one return adult ticket in June?

   b) How much does it cost for one return child ticket in June?

   c) What fraction of the adult's fare is a child's fare?

   d) How much will the return tickets cost for all of Sarah's family?

✈ Choose your travel dates

Lowest fares for May – Sep

May	Jun	Jul	Aug	Sept
Adult £400 ○	Adult £370 ○	Adult £480 ○	Adult £510 ○	Adult £320 ○
Child £200 ○	Child £185 ○	Child £240 ○	Child £255 ○	Child £160 ○

• Prices are quoted in GB pounds (GBP)

2. Sarah now needs to add additional costs including bags, in-flight meals and travel insurance.

   Luggage is charged at £8 per bag.

   How much will it cost for these four bags?

6

A Planning a package

3. In-flight meals cost £6 each.
   a) How much will it cost for Sarah and her family to have a meal flying one way?
   b) How much will it cost for them all to have a meal each way?

   > Include costs for bags, meals and travel insurance.

4. a) Family travel insurance costs £56. How much will all the extras cost?
   b) What is the total cost of flights and extras?

5. Sarah now looks at hotels. She likes two; one inside the Scream Towers theme park and one just outside.

   Sarah finds a brochure for hotel prices per person per night at the Beach Club Resort in the Scream Towers theme park.

   ### Beach Club Resort
   RATES PER PERSON PER NIGHT

Month	May	Jun	Jul	Aug	Sep
Price	£67	£85	£85	£56	£56

   How much will it cost for:
   a) one person to stay one night in the Beach Club Resort in June?
   b) four people to stay one night in the Beach Club Resort in June?
   c) all the family to stay a week at the Beach Club Resort in June?

   > Base your calculation on 4 people for 7 nights.

Sarah also picks up a brochure of prices per person per night at the Sun Resort, which is just outside the theme park. She notices all the prices include breakfast.

Sun Resort
RATES PER PERSON PER NIGHT

Month	May	Jun	Jul	Aug	Sep
Price	£25	£35	£35	£20	£20

6. How much will it cost for:
   a) one person to stay one night in the Sun Resort in June?
   b) four people to stay one night in the Sun Resort in June?
   c) all the family to stay a week at the Sun Resort in June?

7. How much will it cost for the family to stay one week in the Beach Club Resort and one week in the Sun Resort, in June?

8. Sarah now needs to work out the total cost of the holiday including flights, accommodation and any extra costs.

   How much does the two-week holiday cost in total?

   > Use your answers to Questions 4 and 7 to help you.

Unit 1 – Holidaying in Florida

 # Orlando weather

What you need to know

★ Find the mean and range for a set of data and explain what they mean (➡ HD1, p48)

★ Calculate probabilities using fractions, decimals and percentages (➡ HD4, p48)

What you should focus on

★ Write explanations and answers that are clear and easy to follow

1 Sarah uses the internet to find out what the weather will be like when she is on holiday.
   This bar chart shows the average rainfall in Orlando, Florida, in the months from May to September.

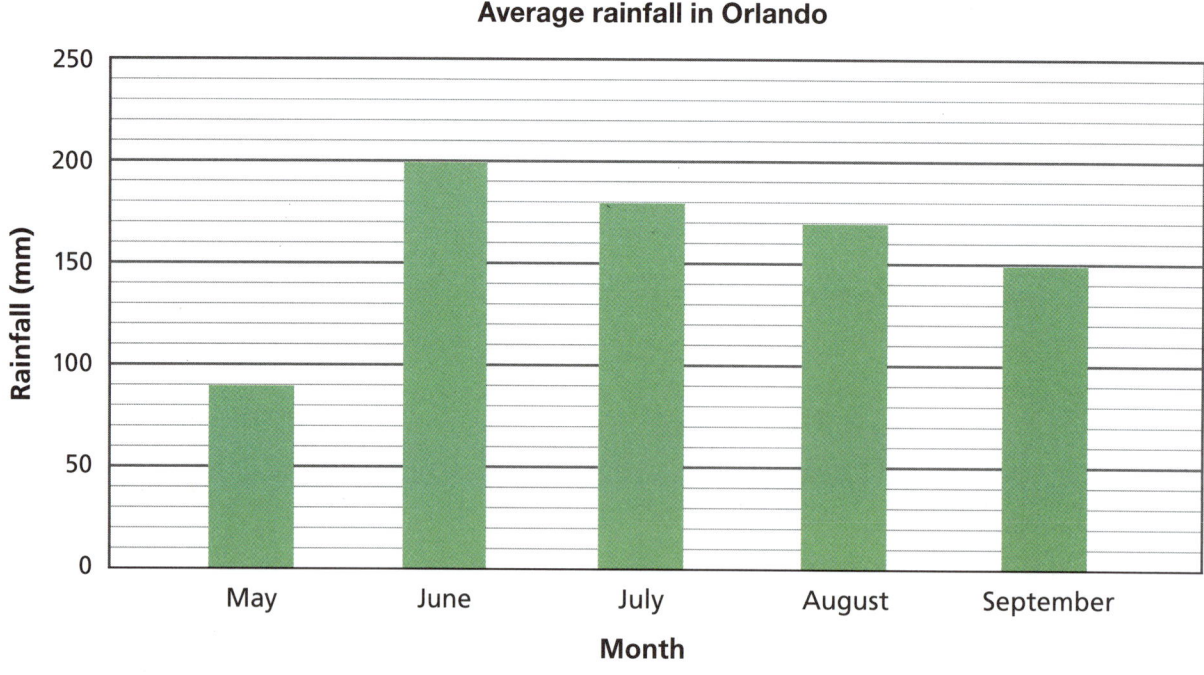

a) Copy and complete the table to show the average rainfall in each month.

b) Which month has the highest average rainfall?

c) Which month has the lowest average rainfall?

d) What is the range of rainfall in these months?

Month	Rainfall (mm)
May	90
June	
July	
August	
September	

B Orlando weather

2. The table below shows the maximum and minimum temperatures in Orlando from May to September.

Month	Maximum temperature (°C)	Minimum temperature (°C)
May	31	19
June	33	22
July	34	23
August	33	23
September	32	22

a) Which month has the highest maximum temperature?
b) Which month has the lowest minimum temperature?
c) Which month has the biggest difference between the highest and the lowest temperature?

3. Sarah is frightened of hurricanes. The table shows the number of hurricanes last year in Orlando. This year is expected to be similar.

a) Which month do you think a hurricane is most likely to occur this year?
b) Which of these months is a hurricane least likely to occur this year?
c) Use the table to estimate the probability of a hurricane occurring in August.

Month	Frequency
May	0
June	1
July	2
August	2
September	5
Total	10

The probability of a hurricane occurring in June is $\frac{1}{10}$

d) Sarah listened to a news report.

> **Daily Blurb reporter:** There is a 50% chance of hurricanes in the month of...

Sarah didn't hear the month. Which was it likely to be and why?

e) She then listened to a different news report.

> **Daily Rant reporter:** There is a probability of $\frac{1}{2}$ that a hurricane will occur in the month of...

Explain why the *Daily Rant* is likely to be saying the same as the *Daily Blurb*.

9

Unit 1 – Holidaying in Florida

 **Changing currency**

What you need to know

★ Add, subtract, multiply and divide whole numbers in your head or with a calculator (➡ NA2, p46)

★ Draw line graphs and frequency diagrams (➡ HD3, p48)

What you should focus on

★ Write explanations and answers that are clear and easy to follow

1 Sarah goes to the Post Office to change money into US dollars ($) for her holiday.

   She has enough money for $50. The Post Office assistant asks what combination of notes she would like.

   a) Copy and complete the table to show some different ways she could make up $50.

$1.00	$5.00	$10.00	$20.00
10	2	1	1

   b) Sarah wants the fewest notes. Which combination of notes will give Sarah the fewest notes?

C Changing currency

2 Sarah would like to buy some souvenirs and has been looking at the Disney Store website in the US.

The lines on the graph show that $7.50 is equivalent to £5.

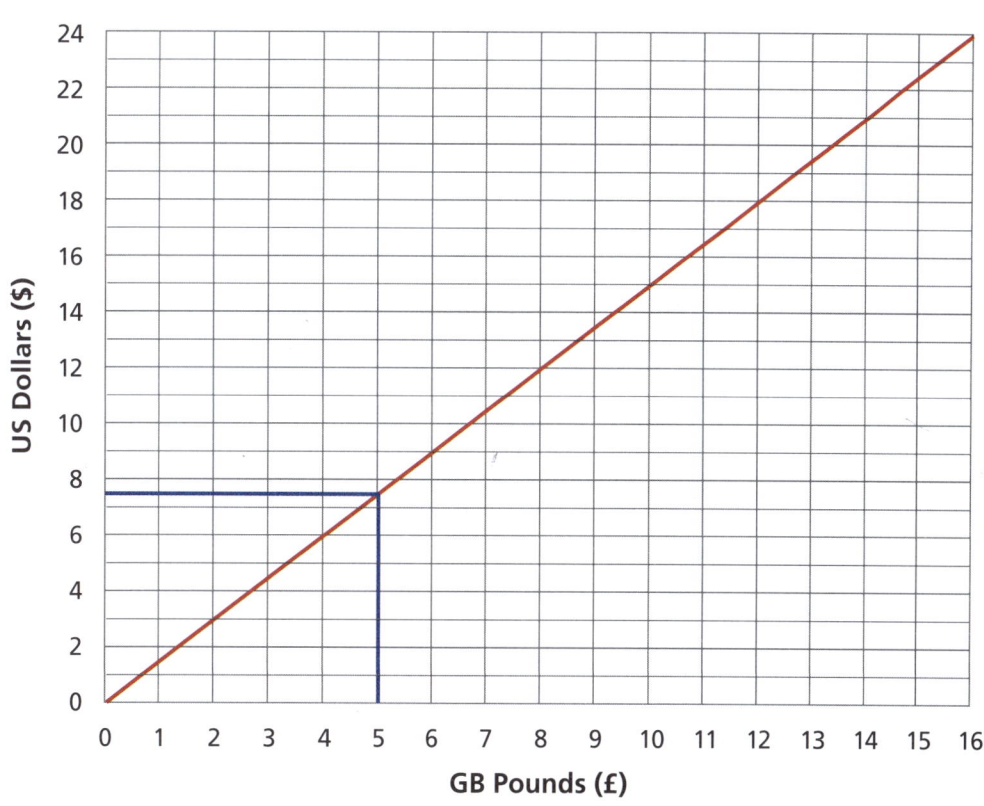

Use the line graph and write down the cost of each of the souvenirs in GB pounds.

a) Mickey Mouse toy $7.50
b) Donald Duck pencil $4.50
c) Minnie Mouse lamp $21.00
d) Goofy mug $6.00
e) Fantasia DVD $24.00

3 Sarah thinks these prices look lower than the ones she has seen in the Disney Store in the UK. She checks the UK Disney Store website and finds prices for the same items.

Copy and complete the table to find the difference in price for each item.

Use answers from Question 2.

Item	UK price (£)	US price (£)	Difference	
Mickey Mouse toy ★★★	£8.00	£5.00	£3.00	BUY NOW IN STOCK
Donald Duck pencil ★★★★	£2.00			BUY NOW IN STOCK
Goofy mug ★★★	£5.00			BUY NOW IN STOCK
Minnie Mouse lamp ★★★	£14.00			BUY NOW IN STOCK
Fantasia DVD ★★★★★	£18.00			BUY NOW IN STOCK

4 Sarah wants to buy each item from the cheapest shop.

What would the total cost be for all five souvenirs? Give your answer in GB pounds.

Unit 1 – Holidaying in Florida

D Scream Towers

What you need to know

★ Find the mean and range for a set of data and explain what they mean (➡ HD1, p48)

★ Multiply whole numbers by 10 or 100 (➡ NA3, p46)

What you should focus on

★ Work out a way to answer a problem set in a real context

1. Sarah's family are planning their trip to the Scream Towers theme park. They want to go for 10 days.

   There are three different types of ticket.

Ticket type	Number of days ticket is valid	Price per day ($) Adult	Price per day ($) Under-16
Quick Coyote	1–5	12	6
Wandering Kangaroo	6–9	10	5
Lounging Lizard	10–14	8	4

   a) Sarah is 13 years old. How much will it cost her for one day as a 'Quick Coyote'?

   b) If Sarah buys two 5-day 'Quick Coyote' tickets, what would this cost altogether?

   c) How much would it cost if she bought a 9-day 'Wandering Kangaroo' and a 1-day 'Quick Coyote'?

   d) How much would a 10-day 'Lounging Lizard' ticket cost for Sarah?

   e) What is the cheapest ticket for Sarah to buy for her 10-day stay?

   f) What is the lowest price that Sarah's family (two adults and two children) would pay to enter the Scream Towers for 10 days?

   g) Why do you think the daily price goes down if people visit the theme park for more days?

2 The souvenir shop shows the prices on the order form used in the shop.

ORDER FORM Scream Towers Souvenirs - Florida

Item	Price	Quantity	Cost
Baseball cap	$2.50	2	
Key ring	$1.25	5	
Lunch box	$4.75	3	
Pencil	$0.20		$3.60
		Total cost of order	

a) Copy and complete the order form. What is the total cost?

b) Sarah's mum paid with $30. How much change should she get?

3 The table below shows how much the family spent during the ten days they visited the theme park. Sarah's brother thinks they spent about the same amount every day. Sarah disagrees.

Day	1	2	3	4	5	6	7	8	9	10
Amount spent ($)	30	30	25	15	20	25	18	27	31	39

a) What was the range of amounts spent?
b) How much did they spend altogether over the ten days?
c) Calculate the mean amount spent per day.
d) Explain whether you think Sarah or her brother was right.

Look at your answers to parts 3 a) and 3 c).

Unit 2 – Smashing smoothies

A Re-writing recipes

What you need to know

★ Add, subtract, multiply and divide without a calculator (➡ NA2, p46)
★ Understand what ratio means (➡ NA6, p46)

What you should focus on

★ Try to work out a problem by using your own ideas

Atiq has been given a smoothie book and a blender for his birthday. The first three recipes in the book are shown below.

1. a) How many grams of fruit will Atiq need to buy to make one Forest Feast smoothie?
   b) How many millilitres of juice are in the Wide Awake smoothie?
   c) In the Chocotastic smoothie, how much does the chocolate spread and banana weigh altogether?
   d) Which smoothie do you think is the healthiest and why?
   e) Which smoothie do you think is the least healthy and why?

B Re-writing recipes

2 a) Atiq starts by looking at the recipe for Chocotastic smoothies.
      Re-write the ingredients to make the smoothie for 2 people.
   b) He would like to make a Wide Awake smoothie for some friends.
      Re-write the recipe for 7 people.
   c) How many Forest Fruit smoothies can Atiq make if he has 750 g of strawberries?
   d) Atiq has the following ingredients for the Wide Awake smoothie.
      What is the maximum number of drinks he can make?

   400 ml cranberry juice
   700 ml orange juice
   600 g melon
   8 lemons

   Think about how much of each ingredient you would need in each drink.

   e) In one Forest Fruit smoothie the ratio of strawberries to raspberries to blackberries is 75 : 50 : 25. Simplify the ratio.

3 Atiq sees an 'Eat 5-a-day' poster encouraging people to eat 5 portions of fruit and vegetables every day.

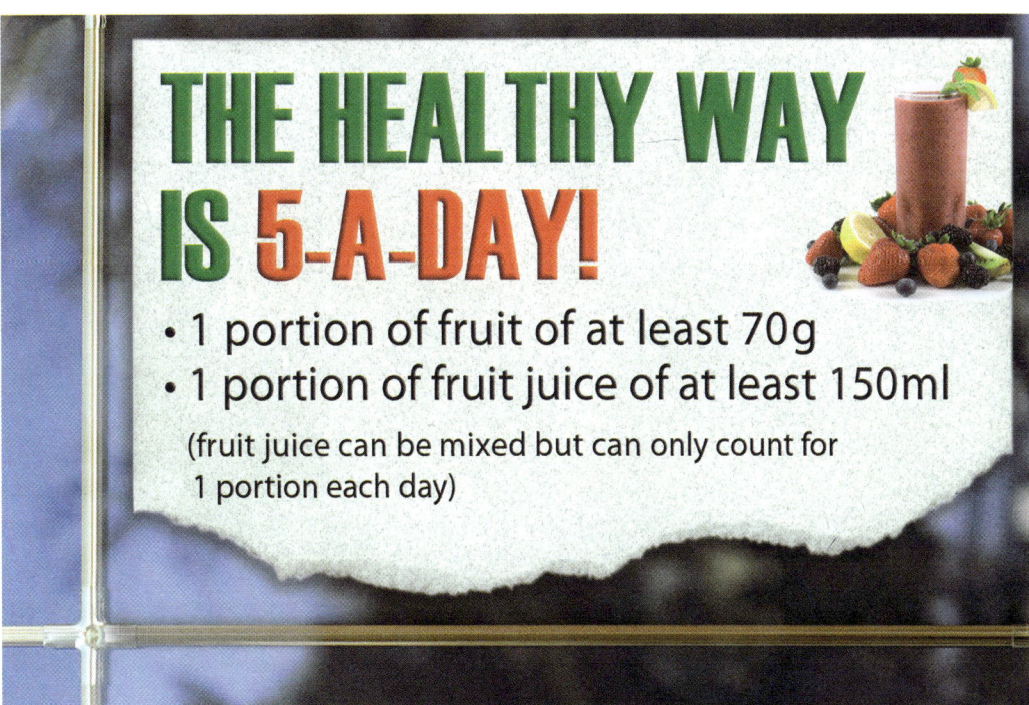

THE HEALTHY WAY IS 5-A-DAY!
- 1 portion of fruit of at least 70g
- 1 portion of fruit juice of at least 150ml
  (fruit juice can be mixed but can only count for 1 portion each day)

   a) Explain how many fruit and vegetable portions are in a Wide Awake smoothie.
   b) Explain why a Forest Feast smoothie would count as 2 portions.
   c) Explain how many portions are in a Chocotastic smoothie.

Unit 2 – Smashing smoothies

B The price is right

What you need to know

★ Add and subtract decimals up to 2 d.p. (➡ NA5, p46)

★ Add, subtract, multiply and divide in your head or with a calculator (➡ NA2, p46)

What you should focus on

★ Use maths skills to solve problems in real situations

Atiq is going shopping for ingredients to make 10 Forest Feast smoothies. He needs:

> 750 g strawberries
> 500 g raspberries
> 250 g blackberries
> 1000 g plain yoghurt

1   A punnet of strawberries costs £2 and weighs 250 g.

   a) How many punnets does Atiq need to buy?

   b) Work out how much he spends on strawberries.

2   Raspberries cost £3.87 for a 200 g punnet.

   a) How many punnets does Atiq need to buy?

   b) Estimate the total cost of the raspberries to the nearest pound (£).

   c) Work out exactly how much he spends on raspberries.

   d) How many grams of raspberries are left over?

B The price is right

3   Atiq spends £3.60 on five punnets of blackberries.
   a) How much does each punnet cost?
   b) He has exactly the correct weight of blackberries. How many grams of blackberries are in each punnet?

4   A 750 g carton of yoghurt costs 98p.
   a) How many cartons are needed for the recipe?
   b) Estimate the cost of the yoghurt.
   c) Work out exactly how much he spends on yoghurt.
   d) How many grams of yoghurt are left over?

5   a) How much does Atiq spend on the smoothie ingredients altogether?
   b) Atiq has a £20 note and two £10 notes. What should he give to the cashier?
   c) How much change will he receive?

   Add together costs of strawberries, raspberries, blackberries and yoghurt.

6   Atiq wants to know if it is cheaper to make smoothies, or to buy ready-made ones from the supermarket.
   a) He spends £8 on the ingredients to make 5 Wide Awake smoothies. How much did each smoothie cost to make?
   b) He sees multipacks of smoothies in the supermarket.

Exotic Smoothies
4 bottles for £6.20

Yummy Smoothies
£4.95 for 3 bottles

Is it cheaper for Atiq to buy Exotic smoothies, Yummy smoothies or to make his own? Explain why.

17

Unit 2 – Smashing smoothies

C Units and measuring

What you need to know

★ Add, subtract, multiply and divide whole numbers in your head or with a calculator (➡ NA2, p46)

★ Read measurements on scales (➡ SSM3, p46)

What you should focus on

★ Try to work out a problem by using your own ideas

1 a) Atiq is weighing bananas to make a Chocotastic smoothie for four people. What do the bananas weigh?

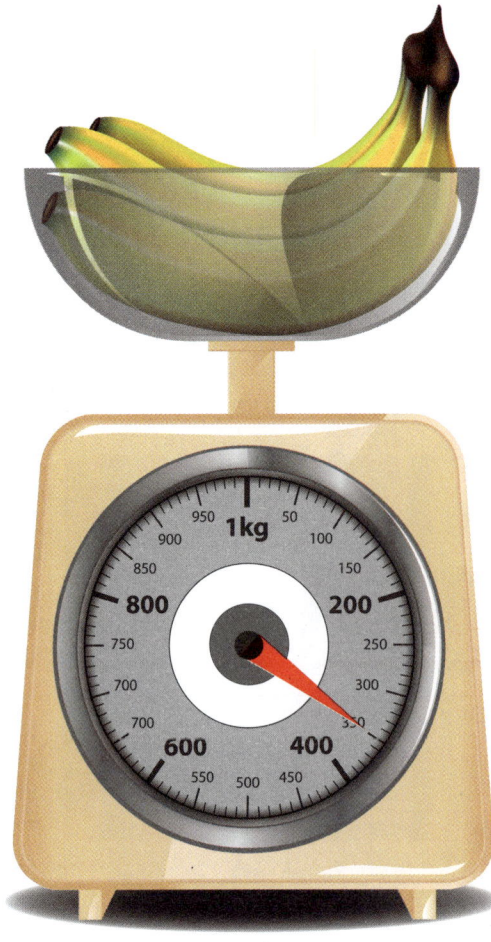

b) He needs 400 g of bananas. How many more grams does he need to add to the weighing scales?

C Units and measuring

2 a) Next Atiq weighs out some chocolate spread. What does the chocolate spread weigh?

   b) He needs 200 g of chocolate spread. How much spread does he need to remove from the weighing scales?

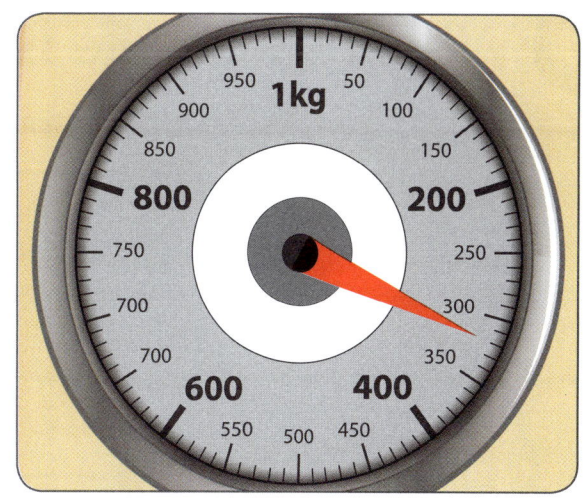

3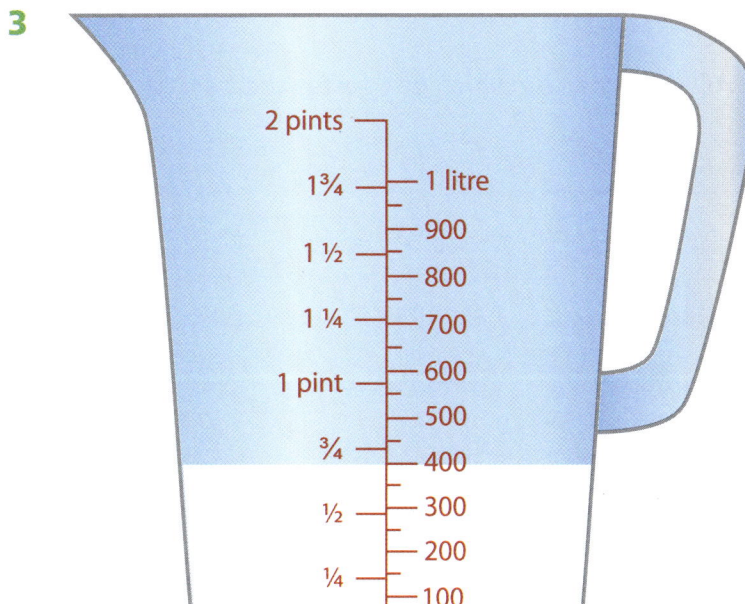

   a) How much milk has he measured out?

   b) Atiq needs 800 ml of milk. How much more does he need to add?

4 Atiq is making 15 Wide Awake smoothies for friends.

   a) The melon weighs 1500 g. How much is this in kilograms?

   b) Fifteen lemons weigh 1.95 kg. How many grams is this?

   c) How much does one lemon weigh, in grams?

   d) A carton of cranberry juice contains $\frac{3}{4}$ litres of juice. How many cartons will Atiq need for the smoothies?

   e) Will there be any cranberry juice left over? If so, how much?

1 kg = 1000 g
1 litre = 1000 ml

19

Unit 2 – Smashing smoothies

 Which smoothie is best?

What you need to know

★ Put discrete data into a frequency table (➡ HD3, p48)

★ Use information from a chart or diagram to come to a conclusion (➡ HD2/HD3, p48)

What you should focus on

★ Write explanations and answers that are clear and easy to follow

1 Atiq asks his friends to try all three smoothies and decide which one tastes the best. He writes down their choices.

Wide Awake	Chocotastic	Chocotastic	Wide Awake	Forest Feast
Wide Awake	Chocotastic	Wide Awake	Chocotastic	Forest Feast
Chocotastic	Wide Awake	Chocotastic	Chocotastic	Wide Awake
Chocotastic	Chocotastic	Wide Awake	Forest Feast	Chocotastic

a) Copy and complete the frequency table to record the results.

Smoothie	Tally	Frequency
Wide Awake		
Chocotastic		
Forest Feast		

b) Draw a bar chart to display the data.

c) How many people did Atiq survey?

d) Which smoothie is the most popular?

e) Which smoothie is the least popular?

f) What is the difference between the number of people who chose Wide Awake smoothies and the number of people who chose Chocotastic smoothies?

D Which smoothie is best?

2 Atiq then asks all his family members which smoothie they like the best. He draws a pictogram to show the results.

a) Which smoothie is the most popular among his family members?
b) Which smoothie is the least popular?
c) How many people in his family did he ask altogether?

3 Write two sentences to compare the choices of Atiq's friends with the choices of Atiq's family.

4 Atiq decides to make new fruit smoothies for his friends and family.
He asks them their favourite flavour and records the results.

Smoothie	Frequency
Strawberry	3
Mango	4
Passionfruit	7
Banana	4
Kiwi	2

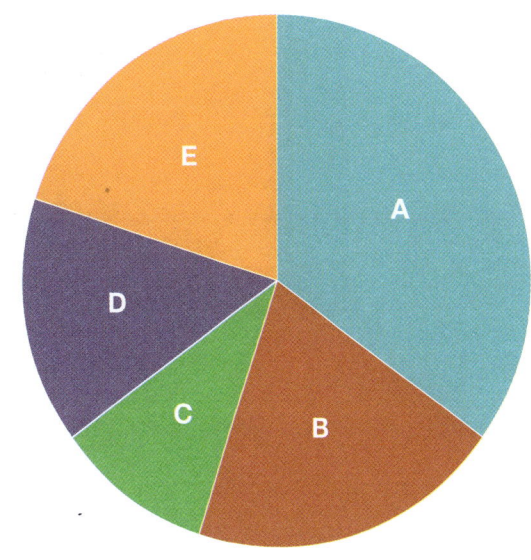

a) Section A on the pie chart represents those people who chose passionfruit smoothies. Explain why.
b) Which smoothies do each of the other sections of the pie chart represent? Explain your reasons.

21

Unit 3 – At the match

A Groundsman

What you need to know

★ Find perimeters and areas of shapes (➡ SSM2, p47)

What you should focus on

★ Work out a way to answer a problem set in a real context

Steve, the groundsman of Hazel Grove United, is getting the pitch ready for the game.

The diagram below shows the range of lengths and widths a football pitch can be.
A team can choose the size of their pitch from the ranges shown.

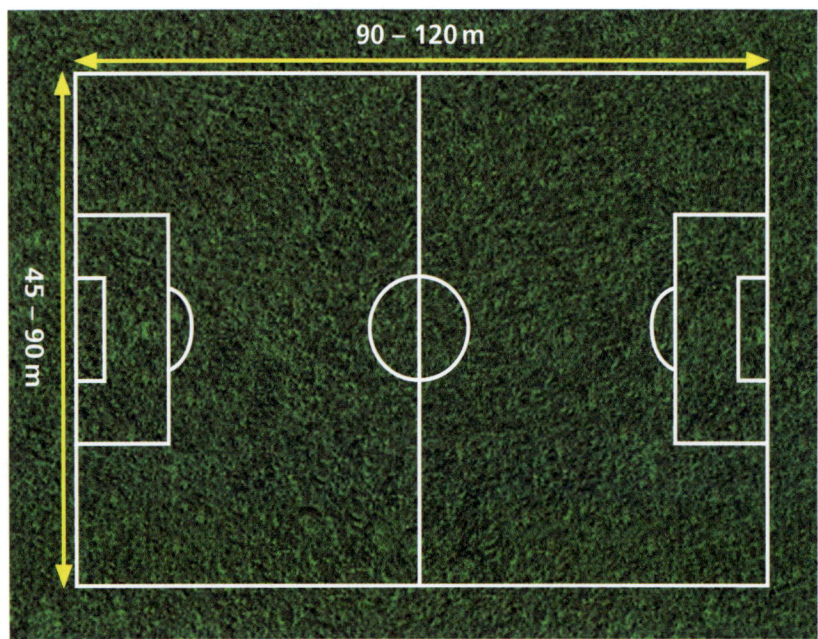

Steve has to re-mark the white lines on the pitch.

1 **a)** How many rectangles does he make?
   b) How many pairs of equal rectangles are there?

2 Steve has chosen to mark out the biggest possible pitch of 120 metres by 90 metres.

   a) Work out the area of the pitch he marks out.

> Area of a rectangle = length × width

22

b) How far did Steve walk to paint the white line around the outside of the pitch?

c) One container of paint will cover 50 metres of white lines on the pitch. How many containers of paint will Steve need for the outside white lines of the largest possible pitch?

Remember to include all four sides.

3 The paint comes in containers.

   a) Work out the volume of the paint container.

   b) Steve's work trolley is 50 cm by 50 cm.
   What is the maximum number of containers he can stand in a single layer on the base of his trolley?

Volume = length × width × height

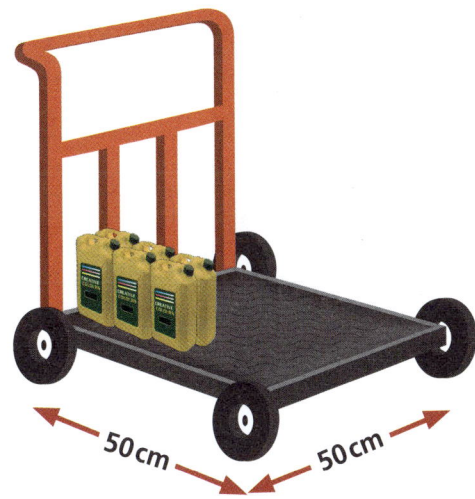

4 Steve finishes marking out the pitch so that Hazel Grove United can warm up for the game. They jog three laps of half of the pitch.

   a) What are the dimensions of half of the pitch?
   b) What distance do they run by doing three laps of half of the pitch?
   c) The team trainer likes the team to run 1000 metres before the game. How many more metres have they got left to run?

Unit 3 – At the match

B The fan

What you need to know

★ Add, subtract, multiply and divide whole numbers without a calculator (➡ NA2, p46)

★ Add and subtract decimals to 2 d.p. (➡ NA5, p46)

What you should focus on

★ Use maths skills to solve problems in real situations

Juan is a fan of Hazel Grove United. He likes to travel to away games, as well as attending home matches.

The table below lists the distances in kilometres that supporters have to travel to watch their team play around the country.

Stockport						
65	Liverpool					
289	331	London				
121	147	187	Birmingham			
207	226	459	323	Newcastle		
14	61	302	134	195	Manchester	
342	366	117	222	536	356	Portsmouth

1 Juan lives in Stockport. How far does he have to travel to:

   a) Liverpool?

   a) Birmingham?

> From Stockport to Newcastle is 207 km.

2 What is the longest distance Juan will have to travel to a match?

3 What is the shortest distance he will have to travel to a match?

4 The kick-off for today's home game is at 12.45 p.m.

Juan takes 25 minutes to get to the car park and 20 minutes to walk to the football ground. He likes to arrive 30 minutes before kick–off.

What time should Juan leave for the match?

B The fan

5. **a)** The first half lasts 45 minutes, plus 3 minutes of extra time.
   At what time does the referee blow for half-time?

   b) Half-time lasts 15 minutes.
   At what time does Juan need to make sure he is back in his seat?

6. Juan visits the refreshments kiosk at half-time.
   Juan has £4.00. How many of the following could he buy?

   a) chocolate bars
   b) bottled drinks
   c) crisps

7. Find the total cost of:
   a) a meat pie, a packet of crisps and a coffee.
   b) 2 hot chocolates and 1 chocolate bar.
   c) a bottled drink and 2 packets of crisps.

8. Juan will only pay £1.25 if he buys a cup of tea and a chocolate bar.

How much cheaper is this than buying the items individually?

9. The match finishes at 2.35 p.m. Juan stays in the ground for an extra 10 minutes.
   At what time does he get back to the car park?

   Look back at Question 4.

25

Unit 3 – At the match

C Kiosk manager

What you need to know

★ Use simple formulae expressed in words (➡ NA7, p46)
★ Find the mean and range for a set of data and explain what they mean (➡ HD1, p48)
★ Work out fractions and percentages of values and measurements (➡ NA4, p46)

What you should focus on

★ Write explanations and answers that are clear and easy to follow

1   Derek, the manager of the refreshments kiosks, is planning how much food to order for the next football match. He looks at the attendance figures for the last five home games.

Opposition	Attendance	To the nearest 1000
Manchester City	20,035	
Fulham	20,928	
Arsenal	26,196	
Liverpool	29,578	
Newcastle	27,264	

a)   Derek rounds the attendance figures to the nearest thousand to help estimate his orders. Copy and complete the table to show the rounded figures.

b)   Put the rounded attendances in size order, starting with the largest.

c)   Use the table to estimate the range of attendances.

d)   Work out the exact range of attendances.

2   Find the mean attendance from the last five games to help Derek decide on the number of orders.

26

C Kiosk manager

3. Derek uses the mean attendance to help him estimate his orders. He knows from past experience that:

   $\frac{1}{2}$ order a cup of tea

   $\frac{1}{4}$ order meat pies

   $\frac{1}{10}$ order chocolate bars

   Write each of these fractions as percentages.

4. The bar chart shows the half-time sales at one of Derek's kiosks.

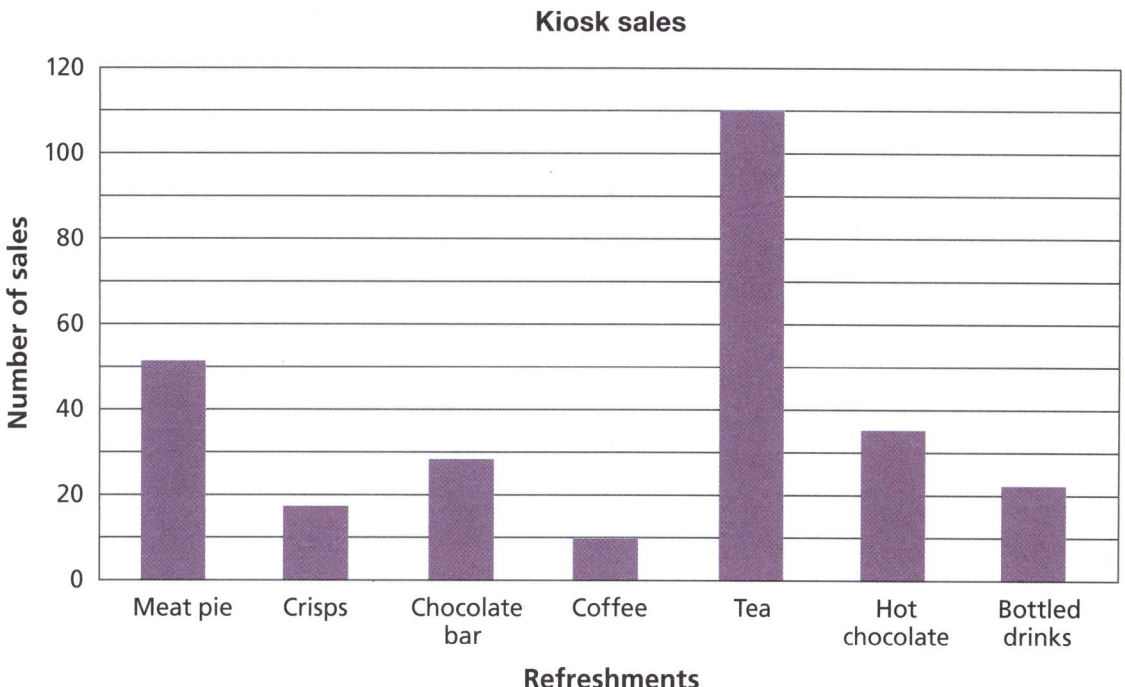

   a) Which item was the most popular?
   b) Which item was the least popular?

5. a) Derek wants to calculate the profit his kiosks are making. He uses this formula to work out how much it costs him to provide cups of tea.

   cost = £0.70 × number sold

   Remember that 70p = £0.70

   Calculate how much Derek spent on providing cups of tea.

   b) Derek sells tea for £1.10 per cup. Use this formula to calculate Derek's income.

   income = £1.10 × number sold

   c) What is Derek's profit for cups of the tea at the kiosk?

Unit 3 – At the match

D Team manager

What you need to know

★ Recognise and use negative numbers (➡ NA1, p46)
★ Find the mean and range for a set of data and explain what they mean (➡ HD1, p48)

What you should focus on

★ Try to work out a problem by using your own ideas

1 Jamie Mack, the manager of Hazel Grove United, is looking at the league table. Hazel Grove United are currently in the bottom half of the league.

Football Table – Premier League – Bottom

Position	Team	Played	Goal Difference	Points
11	Tottenham	30	+2	38
12	Hazel Grove United	30	-5	34
13	Hull City	30	-8	33
14	Sunderland	30	-11	32
15	Portsmouth	29	-10	32
16	Stoke City	30	-1	32
17	Blackburn	30	-8	31
18	Newcastle	30	-13	29
19	Middlesborough	30	-21	27
20	WBA	30	-29	24

Goal difference is worked out by adding the goals a team scores and taking away the goals they let in.

a) Which teams have a better goal difference than Hazel Grove United?
b) How many goals do Hull City have to score to catch up Hazel Grove United?
c) How many goals do Hazel Grove United have to score to catch up Tottenham?

D Team manager

2 Jamie Mack looks at his team's next 5 games.
He writes down what he thinks the scores will be and whether his team will win, lose or draw.

a) Copy and complete the table for him.

Match			Win, lose or draw	Goal difference
Hazel Grove United	0–2	Tottenham Hotspur	L	–2
Hazel Grove United	4–3	Blackburn Rovers		
Hazel Grove United	1–1	Fulham		
Hazel Grove United	2–4	Manchester United		
Hazel Grove United	0–5	Arsenal		
			Total goal difference after 5 games	

Use the number line to help find the total.

b) A win is worth 3 points, a draw is worth 1 point and losing a game gives 0 points.
How many points would Hazel Grove United have after playing these 5 matches?

3 Jamie Mack is considering which striker to play in the next match.
He collects this information after the week's training sessions.

a) Find the overall ratings for each player by adding all their scores.
b) Find the mean rating for each player.
c) Find the range of each player's ratings.
d) Which player should Jamie Mack choose to play in the next game? How did you decide?

29

Unit 4 – Catering

A Market research

What you need to know

★ Put discrete data into a frequency table (➡ HD3, p48)

★ Use information from a chart or diagram to come to a conclusion (➡ HD2, p48)

What you should focus on

★ Write explanations and answers that are clear and easy to follow

Ronaldo is planning to set up his own catering company. He wants to do some research first to find out what people think about food.

He asks people to fill in a questionnaire. He asks them to score foods from 1 to 5 to rate how healthy they think the foods are. Everyone scores each food once. The table shows the results.

Food	'Healthiness' score					Total score
	Very bad 1	2	OK 3	4	Very good 5	
$\frac{1}{4}$ lb flame-grilled cheeseburger	✓	✓✓	✓	✓✓✓✓	✓	
Lasagne		✓✓	✓✓	✓✓✓✓	✓✓	
Chips and gravy from the chippie	✓✓✓✓	✓✓✓	✓	✓✓		
Tuna salad with olive oil dressing		✓	✓	✓✓	✓✓✓✓✓✓	
Grilled fish fingers	✓✓✓	✓✓	✓✓✓✓	✓		
Cheese and tomato pizza		✓✓✓	✓✓✓✓	✓✓	✓	

Tuna total score =
2 + 3 + (2 × 4) + (6 × 5)

30

A Market research

1. **a)** How many people filled in the questionnaire?
   b) Which food did most people think was 'Very good for you'?
   c) What does a low 'Total score' mean?
   d) Ronaldo wants to offer the four healthiest foods. Help him choose which they are by working out the 'Total score' for each food. Explain your answer.

2. Ronaldo then asked:
   What is the maximum you would spend, to the nearest £1, on a meal?
   He got the following results back:

   £8   £12   £15   £7   £9   £8   £11   £17   £25   £19   £13   £7   £6   £19   £12

   a) Copy and complete this frequency table.

Maximum spend on meal				
Up to £5	£6 – £10	£11 – £15	£16 – £20	Over £20

   b) Ronaldo decides to make his complete meals (main plus dessert) cost less than £10. Explain why he chose this price limit.

3. Ronaldo then asked: **What is your favourite food from these choices?**
   He collected the results in this frequency table.

Favourite foods		
Food	Tally	Frequency
¼ lb flame-grilled cheeseburger	IIII IIII IIII IIII IIII IIII II	
Chips & gravy from the chippie	IIII IIII IIII III	
Cheese & tomato pizza	IIII IIII IIII IIII IIII IIII	29
Lasagne	IIII IIII IIII IIII IIII	
Home grilled fish fingers	IIII IIII IIII III	
Tuna salad with olive oil dressing	IIII III	

   a) Copy the chart and complete the frequency column.
   b) What is the least popular food?
   c) Ronaldo decides to include the three most popular foods when he prepares his menu. What are they? Explain how you know.
   d) People voted tuna salad as the healthiest food on Ronaldo's first survey. Ronaldo decided not to put it on his menu after the results of his last survey. Explain why.

31

Unit 4 – Catering

B The company premises

What you need to know

★ Use simple formulae expressed in words (➡ NA7, p46)

★ Find perimeters of simple shapes and areas by counting squares (➡ SSM2, p47)

What you should focus on

★ Work out a way to answer a problem set in a real context

1   Ronaldo is looking for somewhere to base his catering company.

   He wants the premises to have certain features.
   • The building needs to be rectangular in shape.
   • The area of the building needs to be about 40 m² so that it is large enough but still affordable to rent and heat.

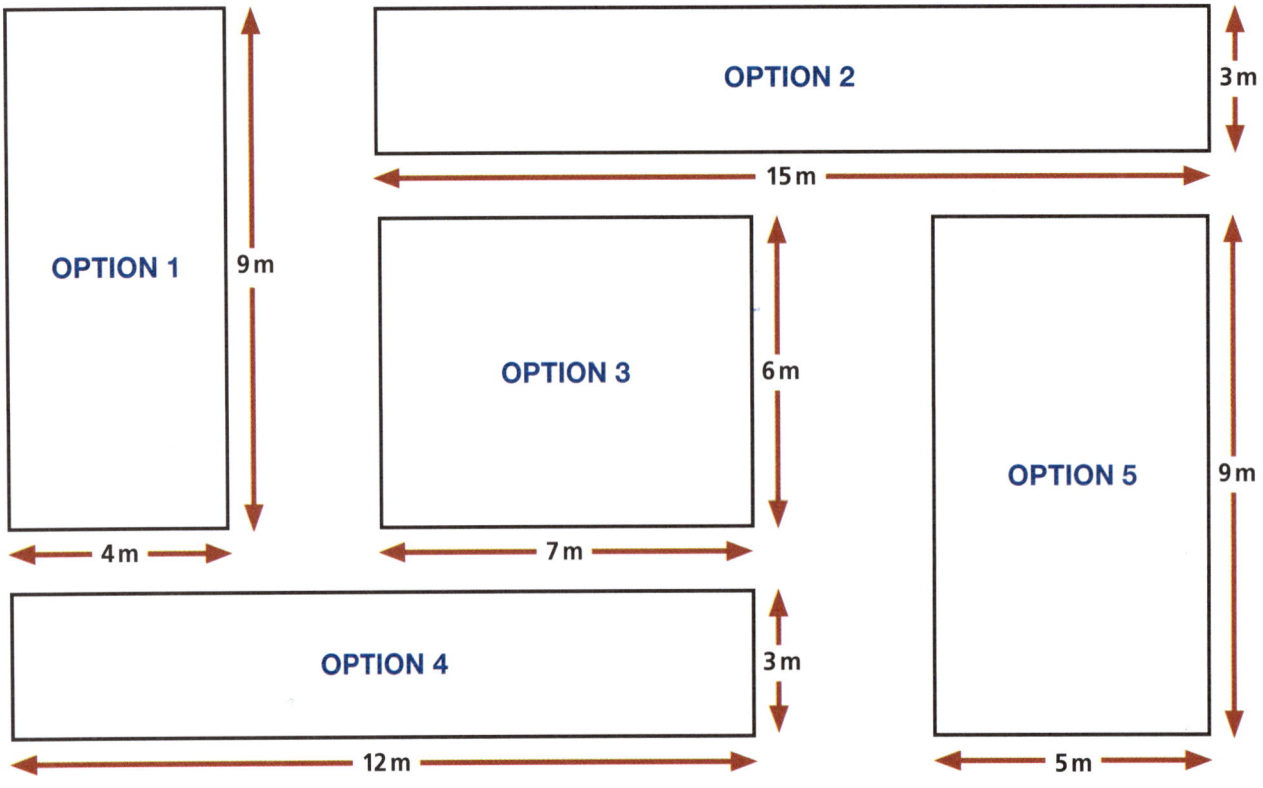

   a) Work out the area of each of the buildings. Show your working.
   b) Which option should Ronaldo choose? Explain your answer.

B The company premises

2 a) Ronaldo needs to give a scale drawing of the building to the flooring company.
He uses a scale of 2 cm = 1 m. Copy and complete the scale table.

Real size	1 m	2 m	3 m	4 m	5 m	6 m	7 m
Size on drawing	2 cm				10 cm		

b) Draw a scale drawing of the building chosen in Question 1 using a scale of 2 cm = 1 m.

c) These three pieces of built-in furniture will be going into the building. Work out the total area of the three pieces of furniture.

Food preparation table (4 m × 2 m)   Large fridge (3 m × 2 m)   Storage cupboard (4 m × 1 m)

d) Ronaldo wants to fit floor tiles only where there is no furniture. What area of the floor will he need to tile?

e) How much will it cost for Ronaldo to have slate floor tiles fitted? Use the flooring price table to help you.

ACME FLOORING CONTRACTORS
For all your flooring needs

PRICE CHART

Finish	Up to 10 m²	11–15 m²	16–20 m²	21–25 m²	26–30 m²	31–35 m²	36–40 m²
Granite	£380	£480	£570	£650	£720	£780	£830
Marble	£330	£430	£520	£600	£670	£730	£780
Slate	£280	£380	£470	£550	£620	£680	£730
Tile	£230	£330	£420	£500	£570	£630	£680

Area of flooring required

3 a) Ronaldo wants to fit new guttering and needs to know how much to buy.
Work out the perimeter of the building.

b) Guttering costs £35 to deliver. The total cost of the guttering can be worked out using a formula.

cost of guttering (in pounds) = number of metres × 5 + 35 delivery

Work out the cost of the guttering for Ronaldo's premises.

33

C Food and nutrition

What you need to know

- ★ Add and subtract decimals up to 2 d.p. (➡ NA5, p46)
- ★ Find the mean and range for a set of data and explain what they mean (➡ HD1, p48)

What you should focus on

- ★ Use maths skills to solve problems in real situations

Ronaldo is looking at the competition for his catering business. He has found two other catering companies and wants to compare their prices.

CREATIVE CATERING

No minimum order required for any dish

Fearsome French Fries	£1.80
Garlic Bread	£1.10
Perfect Pepperoni Pizza	£2.95
Vibrant Veggie Burger	£2.45
Sea-licious Squid Rings	£3.95
Terrific Tuna Salad	£2.45

THE POSH NOSH TROUGH

MINIMUM ORDER 10 SERVINGS PER DISH

Corporate Caviar	£6.95
Princely Pastrami	£5.90
Catwalk Crayfish	£5.40
Voguish Vol-o-vents	£4.20
Royal Roast Potatoes	£3.80
Designer Danish	£3.75

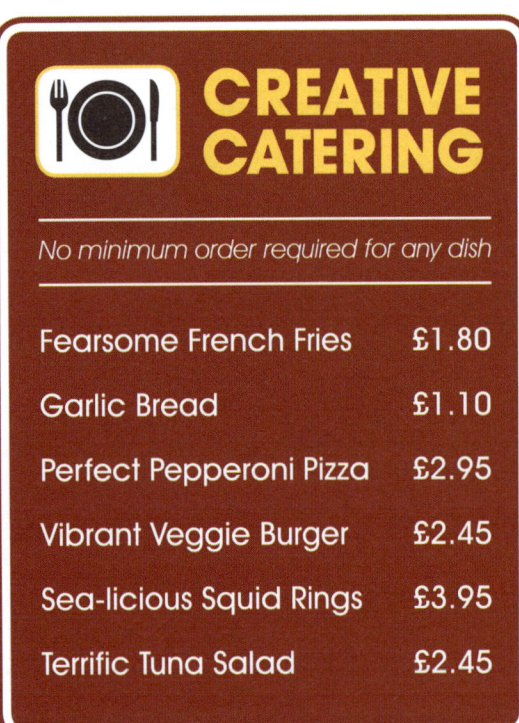

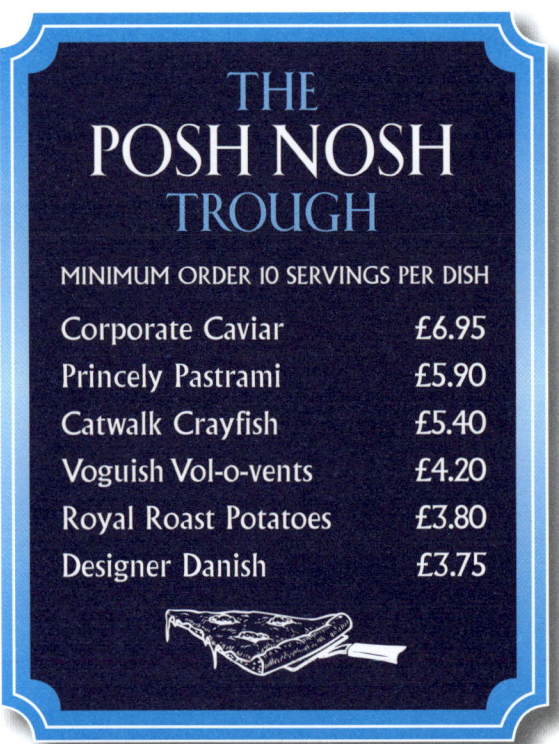

1 a) Re-write the Creative Catering menu in order of price, with the most expensive item at the top.

b) What is the mean cost of items on the Creative Catering menu?

c) How much more expensive is the mean cost of items on the Posh Nosh menu?

d) What would it cost to order eight Terrific Tuna Salads?

e) Ronaldo thinks that the The Posh Nosh Trough will charge £43.20 for eight portions of Catwalk Crayfish. Explain why he is wrong, showing your working.

C Food and nutrition

2   Ronaldo decides to offer the five dishes shown on the menu below, listed in order of cost.

   a) Ronaldo decides that the price of a 'Belting Burger' should be exactly half way between those of 'Long-Ball Lasagne' and 'Dribbling Doughnuts'. What will it cost?

   b) Ronaldo decides to make the range of prices on the menu £2.15. How much will the 'Half-Time Trifle' cost?

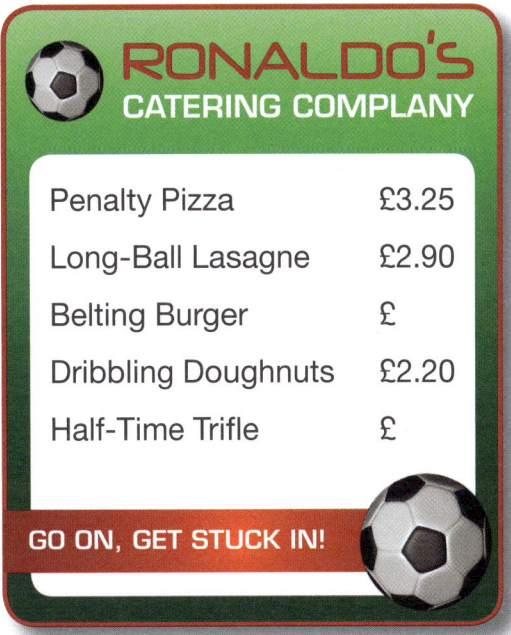

3   Ronaldo sends some nutrition guidelines for three of his dishes to the printers. When he gets them back the names of the dishes are missing. He remembers two facts about the dishes.

Pizza has higher salt content than lasagne

Burger has less protein than lasagne

Which nutrition card is which? Explain your answer.

35

Unit 4 – Catering

 **D Public image of the company**

What you need to know

★ Reflect simple shapes in a mirror line and translate shapes horizontally or vertically (➡ SSM1, p47)

★ Use simple formulae expressed in words (➡ NA7, p46)

★ Find perimeters of simple shapes and areas by counting squares (➡ SSM2, p47)

What you should focus on

★ Try to work out a problem by using your own ideas

1 Ronaldo's girlfriend suggests the name 'Jeepers Eaters' for his company. Here is the logo she creates.

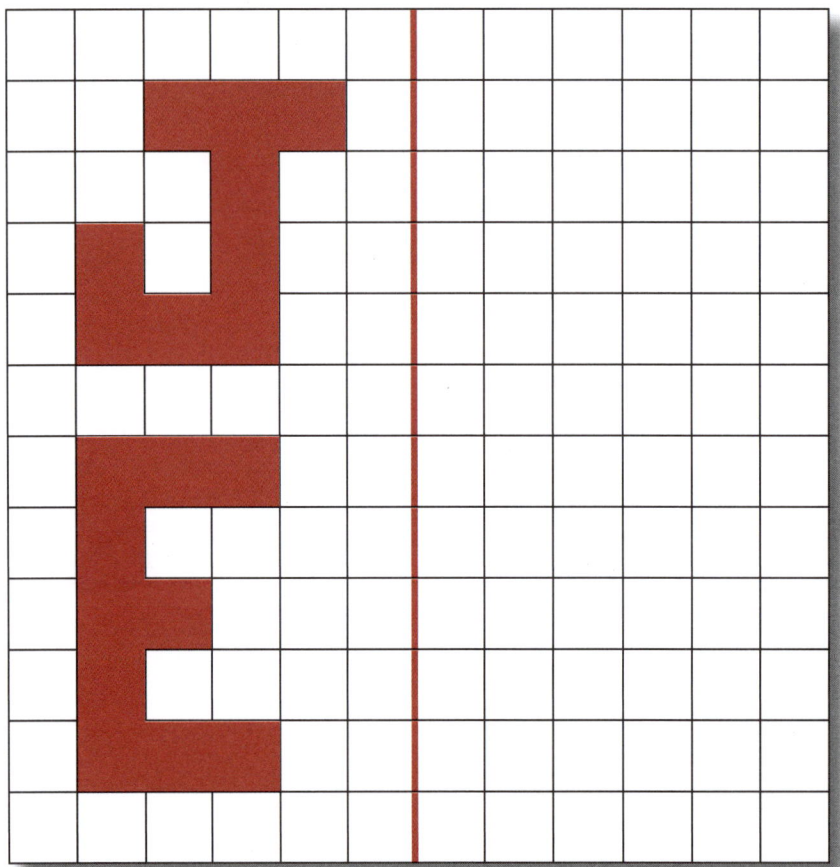

Ronaldo wants to write it backwards so that it looks the right way round when seen in rear-view-mirrors. Copy the letters on to squared paper and then reflect each letter in the vertical mirror line.

D Public image of the company

2 Ronaldo looks at the cost of making letters for the logo. The price depends on the area of the logo.

   a) What is the area in cm² of the 'J' in the logo?

   b) What is the total area in cm² of the letters in the logo?

3 Ronaldo wants to make the full size sign for the 'Jeepers Eaters' building. Every square of the 'J E' logo is to be 1 m² on the real sign.

The sign-maker charges £45 to make each sign and £4.95 for each square metre of the logo.

He uses a formula to work out his prices:

total cost (£) = area × 4.95 + 45

Calculate the total cost of Ronaldo's logo.

You need to use your answer to Question 2 b).

4 The sign-maker says that signs with symmetrical letters are cheaper to make. Ronaldo changes his mind and decides to use the name 'Hunger Team'. The logo will use the letters 'H' and 'T'.

- The logo must have the two letters 'H' and 'T'.
- The letters must each be exactly five squares tall and three squares wide.
- The 'H' must have a horizontal line of symmetry.
- The 'T' must have a vertical line of symmetry.
- The logo can only use vertical and horizontal lines.

   a) Draw the logo on a grid or squared paper.

   b) Calculate the total area of the logo.

   c) Calculate how much it would cost to make the logo into a full-size sign, using the formula in Question 3.

   d) Calculate whether the JE logo or the HT logo is cheapest to make, and by how much.

37

Unit 5 – Bedroom makeover

A Choosing furniture

What you need to know

★ Add and subtract decimals up to 2 d.p. (➡ NA5, p46)

★ Identify simple fractions and percentages (➡ NA4, p46)

What you should focus on

★ Use maths skills to solve problems in real situations

Eva wins a prize of £2000 for a bedroom makeover.

She makes a list of essential items for her room, with prices.

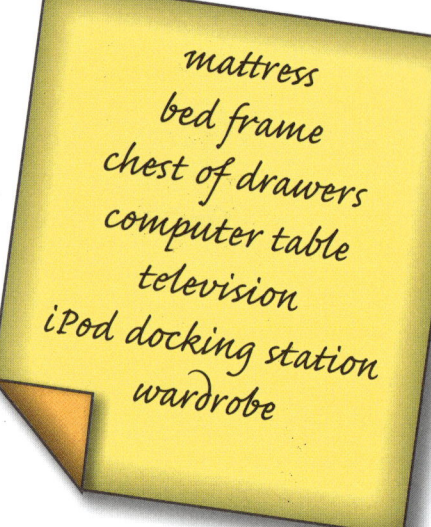

- mattress
- bed frame
- chest of drawers
- computer table
- television
- iPod docking station
- wardrobe

Bed frame £116.00

Mattress £186.75

Wardrobe £282.00

Television £349.00

Chest of drawers £152.00

Computer table £99.00

iPod docking station £200.00

A Choosing furniture

1 a) Estimate the total cost of the seven items.
   b) Work out the exact total of the seven items.
   c) How much prize money is left if Eva buys all seven items?

> Round to the nearest 10.

2 Eva decides to buy some luxury items for her room. She would like a modern chair and a floor lamp.

£159.00

£195.00

a) The lamp is reduced by 50% in a sale. What is the sale price?
b) Eva buys the essential items together with the lamp and the chair. How much does she spend altogether on her bedroom furniture?

3 Eva also has her eye on a mini fridge and a new laptop.

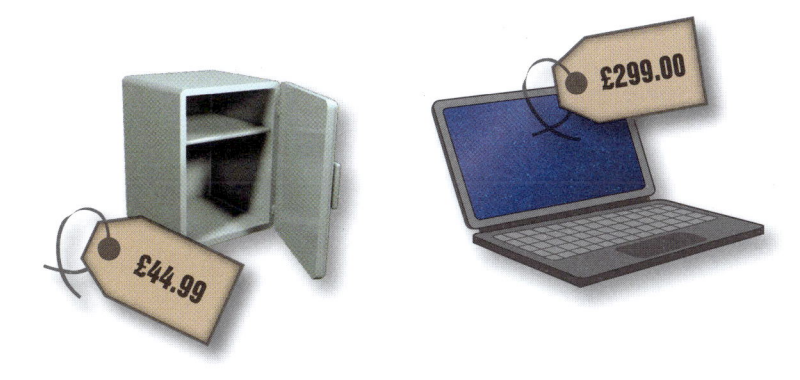

£44.99

£299.00

a) Estimate the extra cost for the mini-fridge and the laptop.
b) What is the exact cost for these two extra items?
c) Eva calculates that she is a little over her budget if she buys the mini-fridge and laptop.
   By how much has she gone over her budget?

> Use your totals from Questions 2 and 3.

4 Eva's mum offers to pay the extra money she needs if she shows her how she has spent her money. List all of Eva's purchases in order of cost.

Unit 5 – Bedroom makeover

B Fitting in the furniture

What you need to know

★ Multiply whole numbers by 10 or 100 (➡ NA3, p46)
★ Find perimeters and areas of shapes (➡ SSM2, p47)

What you need to focus on

★ Try to work out a problem by using your own ideas

1 a) Eva now needs to fit all the furniture into her room. Her bedroom is 3 m wide and 4 m long.

What is the area of Eva's bedroom? (Make sure you include units.)

b) Eva uses a scale drawing to work out the best way of arranging her furniture.
How long and wide is Eva's room in cm?

c) Draw Eva's bedroom to scale, use 1 cm to represent 50 cm.

d) What is the area of your scale drawing?
(Make sure you include units.)

1 m = 100 cm

Use centimetre squared paper.

This diagram shows a plan view of the large items of furniture with measurements.

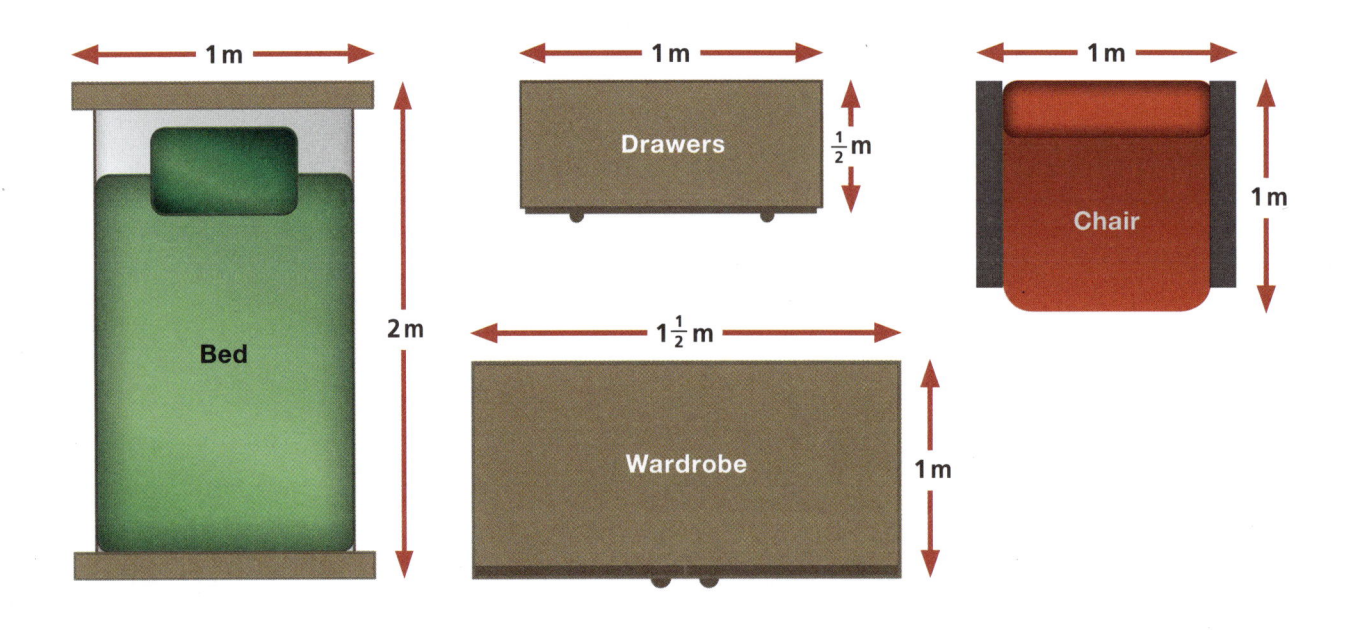

Bed: 1 m × 2 m

Drawers: 1 m × $\frac{1}{2}$ m

Chair: 1 m × 1 m

Wardrobe: $1\frac{1}{2}$ m × 1 m

40

B Fitting in the furniture

2 Write down the measurements of each of the main pieces of furniture, in centimetres.
   a) bed
   b) wardrobe
   c) drawers
   d) chair

3 a) Draw Eva's bedroom furniture to scale, using 1 cm to represent 50 cm.
   b) Cut out these pieces of furniture and place them on your bedroom plan.

4 What is the area of your scale drawings of each piece of furniture?
   (Make sure you include units.)
   a) bed
   b) wardrobe
   c) drawers
   d) chair

5 a) What area of the room is covered with furniture in your scale drawing?
   b) What area of the room is not covered by furniture in your scale drawing?
   c) What does this tell you about the floor space in Eva's room?

6 Eva still has to fit the floor lamp into her room.
   Draw a small circle on your scale drawing to show the position of the lamp. Try to place the lamp near the bed and in a corner.

7 Eva can have a sofa if she has space.
   Draw the sofa to scale. Will it fit in the bedroom?

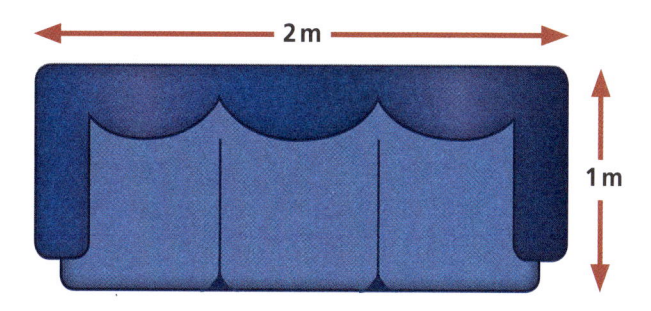

8 Would adding a window and a door in your plan change where you put your furniture? Explain your answer.

Unit 5 – Bedroom makeover

C Painting and decorating

What you need to know

★ Add, subtract, multiply and divide whole numbers without a calculator (➡ NA2, p46)

★ Use simple formulae expressed in words (➡ NA7, p46)

★ Find perimeters and areas of shapes (➡ SSM2, p47)

What you should focus on

★ Use maths skills to solve problems in real situations

Eva's room is 3 m wide by 4 m long and has an area of 12 m^2. She would like a navy blue carpet and has found two shops, both of which sell the same carpet but have different offers.

1

SPECIAL OFFER
COMFY CARPETS
Any carpet for £155. Underlay for £70.
Carpet fitting only £80!

a) How much does the carpet and underlay cost altogether from Comfy Carpets?

b) What would be the cost of the carpet, underlay and fitting from Comfy Carpets?

2 a) How much does it cost for one square metre of carpet and underlay from Smilies Carpets?

b) What will Eva pay for 12 m^2 of carpet and underlay from Smilies Carpets?

SPECIAL OFFER
Smilies Carpets
£10 per square metre.
£6 per square metre for underlay.
FREE Carpet fitting!

C Painting and decorating

3   a) Which is the cheapest place to buy carpet, underlay and fitting?

　　b) How much would Eva save buying from here instead of the more expensive shop?

4   Karl has been hired to complete the painting and decorating. He estimates that it will take him three days do all the painting and decorating. He charges £160 per day plus an initial £50 call-out charge.

wages = 160 × number days + 50

How much will it cost to pay Karl?

5   Karl needs to work out how many tins of paint he needs to buy. First he needs to work out the area of the 4 walls. The room has 2 walls of each of these sizes.

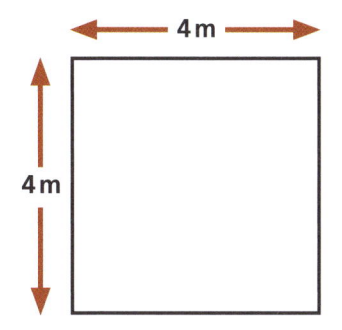

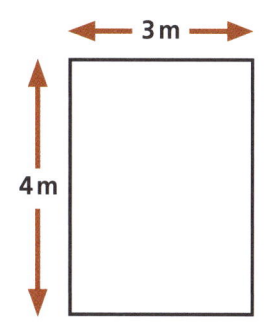

　　a) What is the area of each of these walls?

　　b) What is the total area of all 4 walls?

Area = length × width

6   The bedroom has two walls with a door and window, which do not need painting.

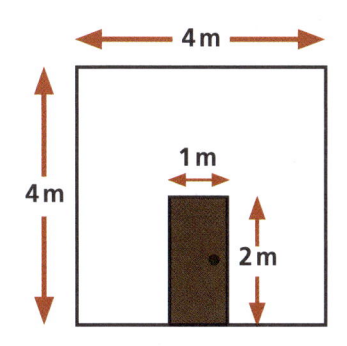

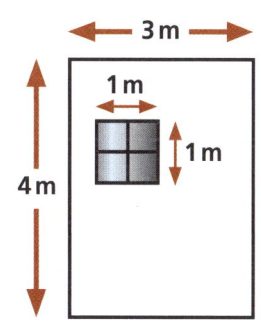

What is the area of the walls that needs painting?

7   Eva buys two tins of paint for £15.99, which will cover an area of 64 m² in total.

　　a) How much do the two tins of paint cost?

　　b) What area will the remaining paint cover after the room has been painted?

43

Unit 5 – Bedroom makeover

D Designing pictures

What you need to know

★ Reflect shapes in a mirror line (➡ SSM1, p47)

What you should focus on

★ Write explanations and answers that are clear and easy to follow

1 Eva is going to make her own pictures for the walls. She buys four 40 cm square canvasses for £6.99 each.

  a) Estimate how much it will cost to buy the four canvasses. Show your working.

  b) What is the exact cost of the four canvasses?

  c) Eva pays with a £20 and a £10 note. How much change will she get?

  d) She is given change in coins. What is the minimum number of coins she could get in change? List the coins.

2 Eva decides that she will only use polygons in her pictures.

  a) Name each of these shapes.

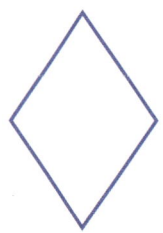

  b) Which of these shapes will she not use?

  c) What family do the three other shapes belong to?

D Designing pictures

3 Eva has chosen polygons that are symmetrical.

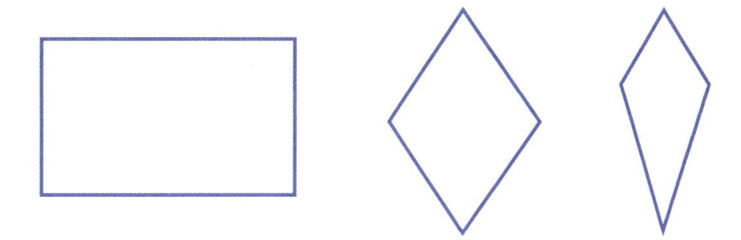

a) Copy the polygons and mark on the lines of symmetry onto the shapes.

b) Mark the equal sides and parallel sides on your three shapes.

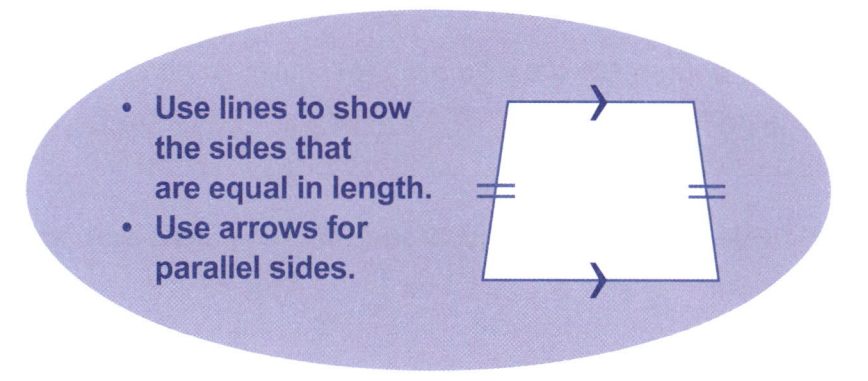

- Use lines to show the sides that are equal in length.
- Use arrows for parallel sides.

Eva creates a design with the three polygons.

a) Trace the design and then reflect it using the vertical and horizontal mirror lines to make Eva's final art work for her bedroom.

b) Does it make a difference which reflection you complete first?

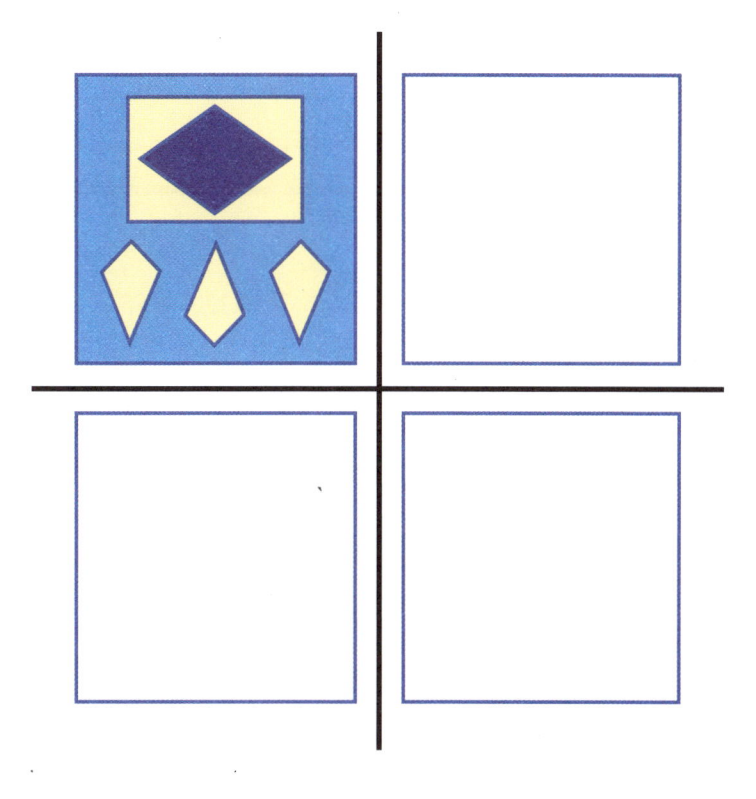

45

Review exercises

Number and algebra

NA1 Understand and use whole numbers and recognise negative numbers in a practical context

The table shows average temperatures in January.

1. Which place has the coldest temperature?
2. Which place has the warmest temperature?
3. Write the cities out in order of temperature, coldest first.
4. What is the difference in temperature between
   a) Hong Kong and Melbourne?
   b) London and Paris?
   c) Paris and New York?
   d) Paris and Moscow?

City	Country	Temp. °C
Berlin	Germany	−1
Hong Kong	China	15
London	UK	4
Melbourne	Australia	20
Moscow	Russia	−9
New York	USA	−2
Paris	France	−3

NA2 Add, subtract, multiply and divide whole numbers using mental methods or a calculator

1. a) 8 + 9   b) 24 + 25
2. a) 18 − 9   b) 34 − 12
3. a) 2 × 14   b) 6 × 34
4. a) 36 ÷ 4   b) 66 ÷ 3
5. a) 322 + 245   b) 650 − 345
6. a) 24 × 18   b) 34 × 12

NA3 Multiply and divide whole numbers by 10 and 100 using mental arithmetic or a calculator

1. a) 8 × 10   b) 17 × 10
2. a) 30 ÷ 10   b) 120 ÷ 10
3. a) 35 ÷ 10   b) 124 ÷ 10
4. a) 124 × 100   b) 245 × 100
5. a) 1200 ÷ 100   b) 2400 ÷ 100
6. a) 2000 ÷ 100   b) 50000 ÷ 10

NA4 Understand and use equivalences between common fractions, decimals and percentages

1. Copy and complete the following table with the equivalent fraction, decimal or percentage.

Fraction	Decimal	Percentage
$\frac{1}{2}$		
	0.25	
		10%
		30%
$\frac{3}{4}$		
	0.4	

NA5 Add and subtract decimals up to two decimal places

Complete the following questions.
1. 0.54 + 1.23
2. 1.54 − 1.23
3. 0.12 + 1.55
4. 1.12 − 1.05

NA6 Solve simple problems involving ratio, where one number is a multiple of the other

Share the amounts in the given ratio.
1. £56 in the ratio 3 : 5
2. £63 in the ratio 4 : 5
3. £72 in the ratio 5 : 7

NA7 Use simple formulae expressed in words for one-step or two-step operations

Use the word formulae to work out the following:
1. Total pay = 6 × hours
   a) when hours = 5
   b) when hours = 8
   c) when hours = 12
2. Total pay = 5 × hours + 10
   a) when hours = 4
   b) when hours = 7
   c) when hours = 10

Review exercises

Shape, space and measures

SSM1 Reflect objects across a mirror line
1 Copy these shapes and reflect them in the mirror lines.

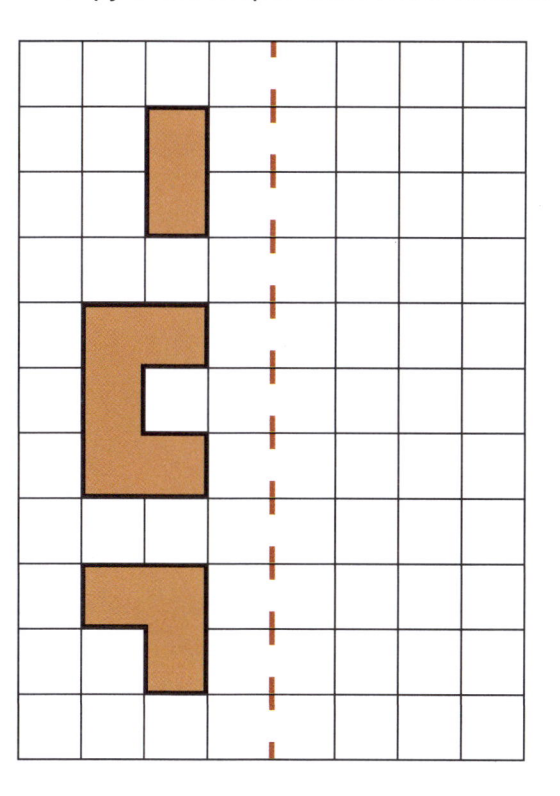

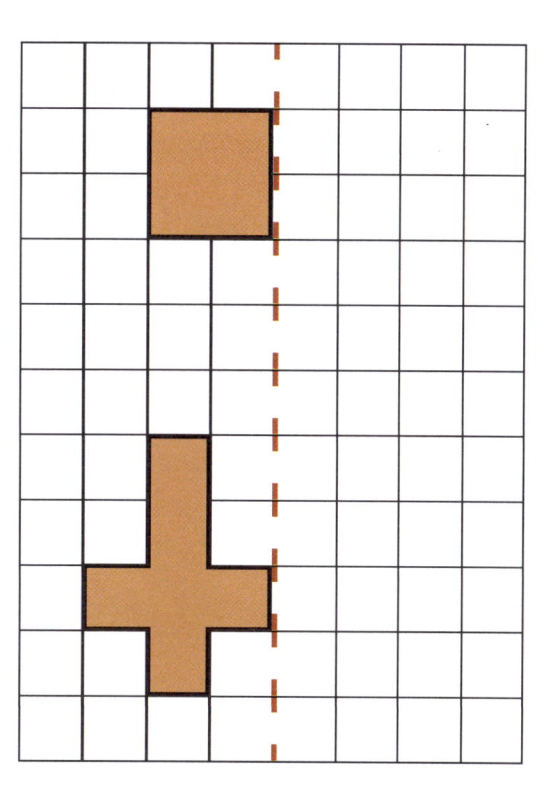

SSM2 Calculate area and perimeter of rectangles
1 Calculate the area and perimeter of these rectangles.

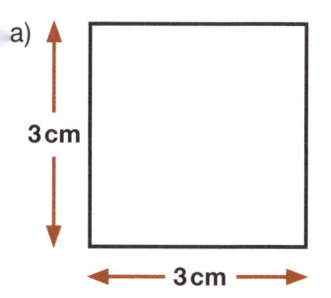

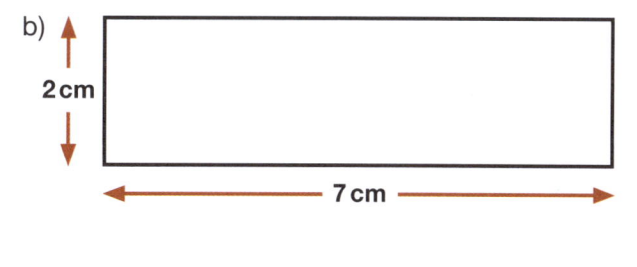

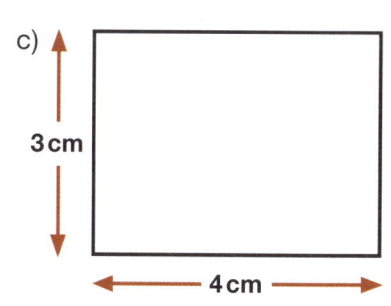

a) 3 cm × 3 cm

b) 2 cm × 7 cm

c) 3 cm × 4 cm

SSM3 Read measurements on scales in a variety of situations
What numbers are the arrows pointing to?

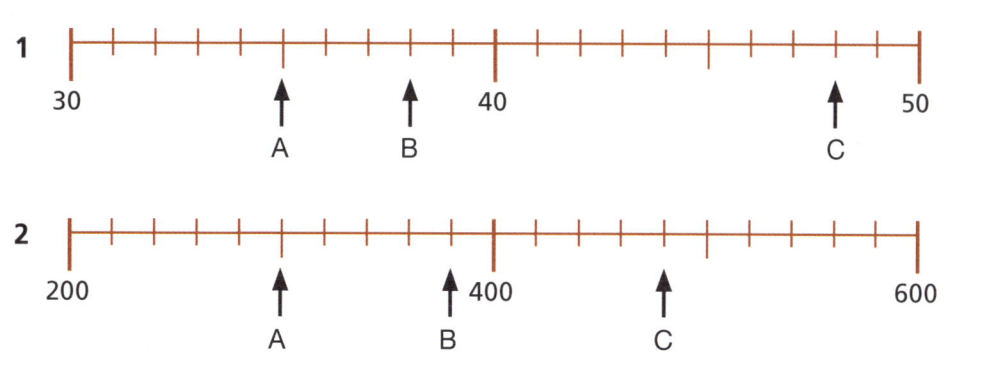

1 Scale from 30 to 50, arrows A, B, C

2 Scale from 200 to 600, arrows A, B, C (400 marked)

47

Review exercises

Handling data

HD1 Calculate mean and range of a set of data

1. Find the mean of the numbers below.
   a) 8, 7, 6, 10, 4
   b) 23, 32, 40, 37, 29, 25

2. The height in centimetres of ten children are shown below.
   132   130   147   133   143   150   136   141   145   143
   Calculate the mean height.

3. The weekly wages of 8 office staff are shown below.
   £180   £155   £210   £150   £300   £220   £125   £260
   Calculate the mean wage.

4. Find the range of each set of numbers below.
   a) 23, 32, 36, 38, 40
   b) 17, 11, 15, 22, 27, 22
   c) 132, 135, 127, 139, 140, 155, 115, 130

HD2 Extract information from tables and charts

The bar chart shows a group of children's favourite crisps.

a) How many children were surveyed?
b) What is the most popular flavour?
c) How many more children liked bacon crisps than prawn cocktail crisps?

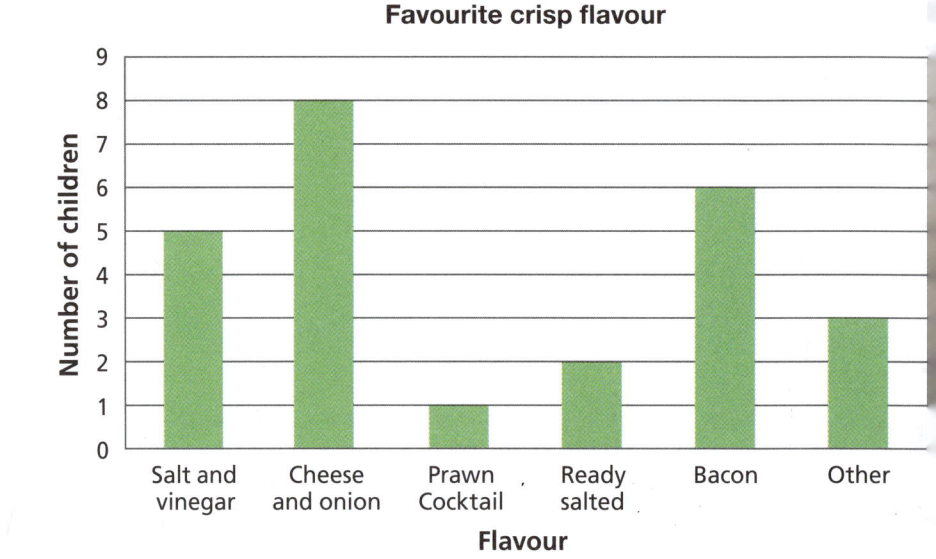

HD3 Record information in tables and charts

1. A student recorded midday temperature in degrees Celsius (°C) every day for two weeks in February.
   11   13   8   10   12   10   13   12   9   11   12   11   13   12

   Copy and complete the frequency table.

Temperature (°C)	Tally	Frequency
8		
9		
10		
11		
12		
13		

HD4 Calculate and compare probabilities using fractions, decimals and percentages

The probability of selecting a green ball from a bag is $\frac{1}{2}$. The probability of selecting a blue ball is 0.3 and the probability of selecting a yellow ball is 20%.

1. Which colour ball is most likely to be picked out?
2. Which colour ball is least likely to be picked out?